The Bathroom Social Media Joke Book

———— • ————

by

Jack Kreismer

RED-LETTER PRESS, INC.
Saddle River, New Jersey

THE BATHROOM
SOCIAL MEDIA JOKE BOOK
ISBN-13: 978-1-60387-091-7
ISBN: 1-60387-091-1

Red-Letter Press, Inc.
P.O. Box 393
Saddle River, NJ 07458

www.Red-LetterPress.com

ACKNOWLEDGMENTS

EDITORIAL:
Jeff Kreismer

•

BOOK DESIGN & TYPOGRAPHY:
Jeff Kreismer

•

COVER:
Jeff Godby

•

INTERIOR ART:
Andrew Towl

•

CONTRIBUTORS:
Kiersten Jacobsen
David Reyneke
Kobus Reyneke

The
Bathroom
Social Media
Joke
Book

Post-A-Pun

There was a two-car accident. The driver of the car that was rear-ended was a dwarf. He got out of his car, looked at the damage and said, "I'm not happy."

The other driver said, "Well, which one are you then?"

•

A rubber band pistol was confiscated from algebra class because it was a weapon of math disruption.

Q: What did Jay-Z call his girlfriend before they got married?

A: Feyonce

•

Here's to the guy who invented Zero- Thanks for nothing!

•

How many tickles does it take to make an octopus laugh?

Ten tickles

•

If you want to catch a squirrel simply climb a tree and act like a nut.

•

A restaurant reviewer accused a chef of plagiarism because he didn't cite his sauces.

•

She was only a whiskey maker, but he loved her still.

Little Johnny @LittleJohnny1n2
To the man on crutches, dressed in camouflage, who stole my wallet ... you can hide but you can't run.

Have you heard about the sword-swallower who was on a diet?

He was on pins and needles for a month.

•

It's difficult to explain puns to kleptomaniacs because they always take things literally.

•

Q: How does Walt Disney World advertise?

A: By word of mouse.

•

The roundest knight at King Arthur's round table was Sir Cumference. He acquired his size from too much pi.

•

I thought I saw an eye doctor on an Alaskan island, but it turned out to be an optical Aleutian.

•

The ladies of the evening were all vegetarians at the brothel sprout.

•

Q: What do you call a fake noodle?

A: An impasta.

•

The butcher backed into the meat grinder and got a little behind in his work.

•

A dog gave birth to puppies near the road and was cited for littering.

A grenade thrown into a kitchen in France would result in Linoleum Blownapart.

•

Two silk worms had a race. They ended up in a tie.

•

Q: What do you get if you cross a pigeon and a general?
A: A military coo.

•

Two hats were hanging on a hat rack in the hallway. One hat said to the other, "You stay here, I'll go on ahead."

•

When the cannibals ate a missionary, they got a taste of religion.

•

I can't believe I got fired from the calendar factory. All I did was take a day off.

tweet

Little Johnny @LittleJohnny1n2
Knock Knock... Who's there? ...
Control freak- Now you say "Control freak who?"

The surgeon was finishing up an operation when all of the sudden the patient wakes up and demands to know what is going on. "I'm about to sew you up," the surgeon says.

The patient grabs his hand and says, "Oh, no you're not! I'll close my own incision."

The doctor hands him the needle and says, "Suture self."

•

Male deer have buck teeth.

•

Pampered cows make spoiled milk.

•

Relationships are a lot like algebra. Have you ever looked at your X and wondered Y?

•

There was a jailbreak and I saw a midget prisoner climb up the fence. As he jumped down, he sneered at me and I thought, "Well that's a little condescending."

Bathroom Break

"A new study found that nearly one out of three people can't resist using Facebook while in the bathroom. I'm just grateful they're not using Skype."
-Conan O'Brien

Maybe you've heard about the new corduroy pillows. They're making headlines everywhere.

•

There's a new stage show about puns. It's a play on words.

•

A will is very simply a dead giveaway.

•

Old limbo dancers never die, they just go under.

•

Singing in the shower is all fun and games until you get shampoo in your mouth- then it becomes a soap opera.

•

I'm trying to think of a Miley Cyrus joke but it's not twerking.

•

Those who get too big for their britches will be exposed in the end.

Little Johnny @LittleJohnny1n2
A cop came to my house and wanted to know where I was between 5 and 6. I told him kindergarten.

Q: What do clocks eat?
A: Mostly hours-d'oeuvres, in minute amounts, but they usually take seconds.

•

Dwarfs and midgets actually have very little in common.

•

Q: What's the best part about living in Switzerland?
A: Not certain, but the flag is a big plus.

•

It was an emotional wedding. Even the cake was in tiers.

•

Q: What do you call a dinosaur with an extensive vocabulary?
A: A thesaurus

•

Time flies like an arrow. Fruit flies like a banana.

•

Bakers trade bread recipes on a knead to know basis.

•

She had a boyfriend with a wooden leg, but broke it off.

•

Those who jump off a Paris bridge are in Seine.

There was once a cross-eyed teacher who couldn't control his pupils.

•

Old power plant workers never die. They just de-generate.

•

And then there was the spider that had its own web site.

•

A cartoonist was found dead in his home, but details are sketchy.

•

Q: What did the coach say to his losing team of snakes?

A: "You can't venom all."

•

Marathon runners with bad footwear suffer the agony of defeat.

Little Johnny @LittleJohnny1n2
Why are there no fat stickmen?

What do you call a country where everyone drives a red automobile?

A red carnation.

•

A cardboard belt would be a waist of paper.

•

Then there was the man who survived mustard gas and pepper spray and became a seasoned veteran.

•

Sign on toy store: Don't feed the animals. They are already stuffed.

•

Q: What do you call a baby monkey?

A: A chimp off the old block.

•

A backwards poet writes inverse.

•

A perfectly spherical pumpkin makes good pi.

•

When the couple bought a water bed, they started to drift apart.

Bathroom Break

Instead of the John, I call my bathroom the Jim... that way it sounds better when I say I go to the Jim every morning. –someecards

A long knife has been invented that cuts four loaves of bread at a time. It's called a four loaf cleaver.

•

The dead batteries were given out free of charge.

•

A hole has been found in the nudist camp wall. The police are looking into it.

•

The little old woman who lived in a shoe wasn't the sole owner. There were strings attached.

•

At first I hated my haircut, but now it's growing on me.

•

A boiled egg in the morning is hard to beat.

•

Whoever invented the "Knock-Knock joke" should get a No-bell prize.

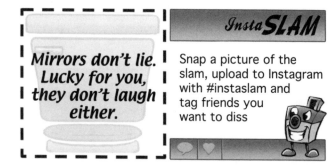

Mirrors don't lie. Lucky for you, they don't laugh either.

InstaSLAM

Snap a picture of the slam, upload to Instagram with #instaslam and tag friends you want to diss

Two cannibals meet one day. The first cannibal says, "You know, I just can't seem to get a tender Missionary. I've baked them, I've roasted them, I've barbecued them, I've tried every sort of marinade known to man. I just cannot seem to get them tender."

The second cannibal asks, "What kind of Missionary do you use?"

The other replies, "You know- they have those brown cloaks with a rope around the waist and they're kind of bald on top with a funny ring of hair on their heads."

The second cannibal exclaims, "Ah, ha! It's no wonder ... those are friars!"

•

In the mid-1800s, the Tates Watch Company of Maine wanted to produce other products. Since the company already produced cases for pocket watches, they decided to market compasses for pioneers who were traveling west. Although their watches were of the finest quality, their compasses were not and were so faulty that people often ended up in Canada or Mexico rather than California.

...And so the origin of the expression, "He who has a Tates is lost!"

She got fired from the hot dog stand for putting her hair in a bun.

•

Even though Catholics in space are weightless, do they have mass?

•

People are choosing cremation over traditional burial. It shows that they're thinking outside the box.

•

Smaller babies may be delivered by stork but the heavier ones need a crane.

•

I was trying to figure out how lightning works when it struck me.

•

The ancient Romans only gathered once a month because that was enough forum.

Little Johnny @LittleJohnny1n2
I changed my car horn to gun shot sounds. People move out of the way much faster now.

There was a big paddle sale at the boat store. It was quite an oar deal.

•

I've always pictured myself taking selfies.

•

A guy goes to his friend's costume party with nothing but a naked girl on his back. "What on earth are you supposed to be?" his friend asks.

"I'm a snail."

"What? How can you be a snail when all you've got is that naked girl on your back?"

"That's not any naked girl, pal," his friend says. "That's Michelle."

•

Historians found that William Tell and his family were avid bowlers. However, all the league records were destroyed in a fire. Unfortunately, we'll never know for whom the Tells bowled.

•

The guy's bakery store burned down last night and now his business is toast.

Bathroom Break

Graffiti on Public Bathroom Stall:
"Beware of Limbo Dancers"

It's tough to do inventories in Afghanistan because of the tally ban.

•

The other day I held the door open for a clown thinking it was a nice jester.

•

John Deere's manure spreader is the only equipment the company won't stand behind.

•

A marine biologist created a species of genetically engineered dolphins that could live forever if they were fed a steady diet of seagulls. One day his supply of the birds ran out, so he went out to trap some more. On the way back, he spied two lions napping on the road. Afraid to wake the sleeping beasts, he gingerly stepped over them.

The authorities caught him in the act, arrested him and charged him with transporting gulls across sedate lions for immortal porpoises.

tweet

Little Johnny @LittleJohnny1n2
I'm so poor I can't even pay attention.

Have you ever tried to eat a clock? It's very time consuming.

•

Police were called to a daycare where a three-year-old was resisting a rest.

•

I used to have a fear of hurdles, but I got over it.

•

Don't trust people that do acupuncture. They're back stabbers.

•

Atheists don't solve exponential equations because they don't believe in higher powers.

•

A man ran into the doctor's office shouting, "Doctor! Doctor! I think I'm shrinking!"

The doctor responded, "Now, calm down. You'll just have to be a little patient."

•

A relief map shows where the restrooms are.

•

Did you hear about the crime that happened in a parking garage? It was wrong on so many levels.

•

I think Santa's moved to Brazil. All our presents came from Amazon this year.

•

A Freudian slip is when you say one thing but mean your mother.

Facebook Funnies

"Just think- without Facebook, you'd have to call 382 of your friends every night to let them know you're going to bed." -Nancy O'Brien

•

"I've invented Twofacebook, the antisocial network. You start being friends with the entire world and defriend people one by one."
-Andy Borowitz

•

"The two biggest websites right now are Wikipedia, where you go to learn about things you care about, and Facebook, where you go to learn about people you stopped caring about years ago." -Craig Ferguson

•

"I now pronounce you man and wife. You may update your Facebook status." -Anonymous

Little Johnny @LittleJohnny1n2
Philosophy according to a skunk:
I stink, therefore I am.

"A new Facebook app is coming out that will remind users exactly what they were doing a year ago from that day. Nine times out of 10, the answer will be 'wasting your time on Facebook.'" -Conan O'Brien

•

"President Obama wants to get Americans back to what we do best. He wants teachers teaching, police policing, firemen fighting fires, and the rest of us checking Facebook." -Jimmy Kimmel

•

"Andy Warhol said that in the future everyone will be famous for 15 minutes. Facebook is exactly like that except you're not really famous and your 15 minutes goes on forever." -Craig Ferguson

•

"There's a new iPhone app that lets you call your Facebook friends from your phone. Of course, I only got on Facebook so I wouldn't have to call these people." -Jimmy Fallon

•

"I hear YouTube, Twitter and Facebook are merging to form a super Social Media site- YouTwitFace." -Conan O'Brien

•

"Facebook should have a limit on how many times you can change your relationship status. After three, it should default to 'unstable'." -Anonymous

"I'm going to change my name on Facebook to 'Benefits', so that when you add me, it will say, "You are now friends with benefits."
-Anonymous

•

Your reluctance to put me in a Google Plus circle makes me question our Facebook friendship.
-someecards

•

Can you imagine if Facebook and Twitter just decided to shut down and you see all these confused people coming out of their house squinting at the sun! -LOLME.com

•

"My ex and I had a very amicable divorce. I know this because when I wrote the Facebook status 'I'm getting a divorce,' he was the first one to click 'Like.'" -Giulia Rozzi

tweet

Little Johnny @LittleJohnny1n2
I'd take Cap'n Crunch more seriously if his eyebrows weren't on his hat.

Life's Big Questions

…Social media conversation starters

• If a cow laughed, would milk come out of her nose?

• If a jogger runs at the speed of sound, can he still hear his iPod?

• If our knees bent the other way, what would a chair look like?

• Is there a time limit on fortune cookie predictions?

• Do you need a silencer if you are going to shoot a mime?

• If you have 24 odds and ends on a table, and 23 fall off, what do you have left, an odd or an end?

• Have you ever imagined a world with no hypothetical situations?

• If you are cross-eyed and dyslexic at the same time, would you see okay?

• When they finish making styrofoam, what do they package it in?

• Since bread is square, then why is sandwich meat round?

• When cheese gets its picture taken, what does it say?

• If an ambulance is on its way to save someone, and it runs someone over, does it stop to help them?

• How come there are no 'B' batteries?

• If man evolved from monkeys, how come we still have monkeys?

• What is a picture of a thousand words worth?

• In the song *Yankee Doodle*, is he calling the horse or the feather "Macaroni"?

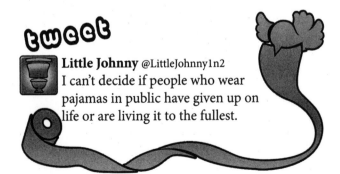

tweet

Little Johnny @LittleJohnny1n2
I can't decide if people who wear pajamas in public have given up on life or are living it to the fullest.

Post-A-Quote

"Don't get mad. Don't get even. Just get elected, then get even." -James Carville

"Never purchase beauty products in a hardware store." -Miss Piggy

"I don't plan to grow old gracefully. I plan to have facelifts until my ears meet." -Rita Rudner

"I like to play chess with bald men in the park, although it's hard to find 32 of them."
-Emo Phillips

"My therapist told me the way to achieve true inner peace is to finish what I start. So far I've finished two bags of M&Ms and a chocolate cake. I feel better already." -Dave Barry

"Marry an orphan: You'll never have to spend boring holidays with the in-laws." -George Carlin

"If I had to describe myself in one word, it would be 'bad at following directions.'" -Matt Roller

"Pie can't compete with cake. Put candles in a cake, it's a birthday cake. Put candles in a pie, and somebody's drunk in the kitchen."
-Jim Gaffigan

tweet

Little Johnny @LittleJohnny1n2
I found a Justin Bieber concert ticket nailed to a tree, so I took it! You never know when you might need a nail.

"I went into a French restaurant and asked the waiter, 'Have you got frog's legs?' He said, 'Yes,' so I said, 'Well hop into the kitchen and get me a cheese sandwich." -Tommy Cooper

"I've been hiding from exercise. I'm in the Fitness Protection Program." -yourecards

"I have opinions- strong opinions -but I don't always agree with them." -George W. Bush

"I got my first bikini. It's a three piece: it's a top, a bottom, and a blindfold for you."
-Wendy Liebman

"It's great to be a godmother. She calls me 'God' for short." -Ellen DeGeneres

"A Vatican cardinal said Jesus was the original tweeter. I don't know how popular he was. He only had 12 followers." -Conan O'Brien

"When I was a kid, we had a quicksand box in our backyard. I was an only child, eventually."
-Steven Wright

"Everyone is on this low-fat craze now. The Mayo Clinic just changed its name to the Balsam Vinaigrette Clinic." -Buzz Nutley

"My brothers would never let me play with them, so to get back at them I put Vaseline on the Twister mat. Left arm, BROKEN!" -Brian Regan

"I was diagnosed with antisocial behavior disorder, so I joined a support group. We never meet." -Craig Sharf

"When I was a kid in Houston, we were so poor we could only afford two letters, so we called ourselves po'." -George Foreman

"Kissing is just pushing your lips against the sweet end of 66 feet of intestines." -Drew Carey

"After 12 years of therapy my psychiatrist said something that brought tears to my eyes. He said, 'No hablo ingles.'" -Ronnie Shakes

Congrats! I heard you took an IQ test and the results were negative.

InstaSLAM

Snap a picture of the slam, upload to Instagram with #instaslam and tag friends you want to diss

"If at first you don't succeed... so much for skydiving." -Henny Youngman

"We need a 12-step group for compulsive talkers. They would call it On Anon Anon." -Paula Poundstone

"Never, under any circumstances, take a sleeping pill and a laxative on the same night." -Dave Barry

"Instead of getting married again, I'm going to find a woman I don't like and just give her a house." -Rod Stewart

"They always say that Albert Einstein was a genius. Then how come when anyone ever calls you that, it's an insult? 'You don't know where you parked the car? Good job, Einstein.' I don't think we're honoring that man properly by using his name in vain in parking lots." -Brian Regan

Bathroom Break

"When a society has to resort to the lavatory for its humor, the writing is on the wall." -Alan Bennett

"A lot of times, I'll drive for like 10 miles with the emergency brake. That doesn't say a lot for me, but it really doesn't say a lot for the emergency brake." -Mitch Hedberg

"I like to stand near ATM machines, and when somebody types in their pin number, I go, 'Got it!' And then I run away." -Demetri Martin

"I wish I had a twin, so I could know what I'd look like without plastic surgery." -Joan Rivers

"We came up with Earth Day so we would have one day every year that would remind us what planet we were living on." -Lewis Black

"I was raised as an only child, which really annoyed my sister." -Will Marsh

tweet

Little Johnny @LittleJohnny1n2
How many divorced men does it take to change a light bulb? It doesn't matter. They never get the house anyway.

"Why doesn't the fattest man in the world become a hockey goalie?" -Steven Wright

"I buy books on suicide at bookstores. You can't get them at the library, because people don't return them." -Kevin Nealon

"When I was a kid I used to pray every night for a new bike. Then I realized that the Lord doesn't work that way, so I stole one and asked him to forgive me." -Peter Kay

"I had a friend who was a clown. When he died, all his friends went to the funeral in one car." -Steven Wright

"My children love my mother, and I tell my children, 'That is not the same woman I grew up with… That is an old woman trying to get into heaven now.'" -Bill Cosby

"You have to remember one thing about the will of the people: it wasn't that long ago that we were swept away by the Macarena." -Jon Stewart

"Today I will live in the moment…unless it's unpleasant, in which case I will eat a cookie." -Cookie Monster

"Sometimes I'm afraid of bears. Sometimes I'm not. I must be bipolar." -Peter Sasso

"Dogs are the leaders of the planet. If you see two life forms, one of them's making a poop, the other one's carrying it for him, who would you assume is in charge?" -Jerry Seinfeld

"It is generally agreed that 'Hello' is an appropriate greeting because if you entered a room and said 'Goodbye,' it could confuse a lot of people." -Dolph Sharp

"I used to work at McDonald's making minimum wage. You know what that means when someone pays you minimum wage? You know what your boss was trying to say? It's like, 'Hey, if I could pay you less, I would, but it's against the law.'" -Chris Rock

tweet

Little Johnny @LittleJohnny1n2
Raisin cookies that look like chocolate chip cookies is one of the reasons I have trust issues.

"Based on what you know about him in history books, what do you think Abraham Lincoln would be doing if he were alive today? (1) Writing his memoirs of the Civil War. (2) Advising the President. (3) Desperately clawing at the inside of his coffin." -David Letterman

"Balding African-American men look cool when they shave their heads, whereas balding white men look like giant thumbs." -Dave Barry

"It's strange, isn't it? You stand in the middle of a library and yell 'aaaaagghhhh' and everyone just stares at you. But you do the same thing on an airplane, and everyone joins in." -Tommy Cooper

"All of the people in my building are insane. The lady across the hall tried to rob a department store... with a pricing gun. She said, 'Give me your money, or I'm marking down everything in the store.'" -Steven Wright

Bathroom Break

How did the female toilet break up with the male toilet?

She sent him a Dear John letter.

"I have often wanted to drown my troubles, but I can't get my wife to go swimming."
-Jimmy Carter

"When you have to get up at 7:00, 6:59 is the worst part of the day."
-Charlie Brown

"There is one thing I would break up over, and that is if she caught me with another woman. I won't stand for that." -Steve Martin

"I've been on so many blind dates, I should get a free dog." -Wendy Liebman

"Guys are lucky because they get to grow mustaches. I wish I could. It's like having a little pet for your face." -Anita Wise

tweet

Little Johnny @LittleJohnny1n2
At what age is it appropriate to tell my dog that he's adopted?

"I phoned my dad to tell him I had stopped smoking. He called me a quitter." -Steven Pearl

"An escalator can never break; it can only become stairs." -Mitch Hedberg

"If you're working out in front of a mirror and watching your muscles grow, your ego has reached a point where it is now eating itself. That's why I believe there should be a psychiatrist at every health club, so that when they see you doing this, they will take you away for a little chat." -Lewis Black

"I have little feet because nothing grows in the shade." -Dolly Parton

"How come aspirins are packed in childproof containers, but bullets just come in a box?" -Jay Leno

"Why do they bother saying raw sewage? Do some people cook the stuff?" -George Carlin

"Do Lipton employees take coffee breaks?" -Steven Wright

"Should not the Society of Indexers be known as 'Indexers, Society of, The'?" -Keith Waterhouse

"What are perfect strangers? Do they have perfect hair? Do they dress perfectly?"
-Ellen DeGeneres

"At the ballet you see girls dancing on their tiptoes. Why don't they just get taller girls?"
-Greg Ray

"Never play peekaboo with a child on a long plane trip. There's no end to the game. Finally, I grabbed him by the bib and said, 'Look, it's always gonna be me!'" -Rita Rudner

"I got my hair highlighted because I felt that some strands were more important than others."
-Mitch Hedberg

"Most people look at the glass as half empty or half full. I look at it as too big." -George Carlin

tweet

Little Johnny @LittleJohnny1n2
Anyone actually ever slipped on a banana peel? Was it funny, or just horrifying?

"Who was the first person to drink milk, and what were they thinking? 'Ooh boy, I can't wait till those calves get done so I can get me a shot of that.'" -Jerry Seinfeld

"French fries. I love them. Some people are chocolate and sweets people. I love French fries. That and caviar." -Cameron Diaz

"If bankers can count, how come they always have ten windows and two tellers?" -Milton Berle

"Man was made at the end of a week's work when God was tired." -Mark Twain

"The insurance man told me that the accident policy covered falling off the roof but not hitting the ground." -Tommy Cooper

"I used to have a dog. And he was a good dog. But these days, he'd be a 'Canine American.' " -A. Whitney Brown

Bathroom Break

What do you call an igloo without a toilet?

An ig.

"Women...can't live with 'em...pass the beer nuts." -Norm Peterson, *Cheers*

"I know God will not give me anything I can't handle. I just wish that He didn't trust me so much." -Mother Teresa

"Sesame Street Workshop announced that they have laid off 60 workers. News of the firings was brought to the employees by the letters F and U." -Tina Fey, on *Saturday Night Live*

"After thirty, a body has a mind of its own." -Bette Midler

"My wife left me and ran off with my best friend. Now I don't have a dog anymore." -Rodney Dangerfield

tweet

Little Johnny @LittleJohnny1n2
I remember the first time I saw a universal remote control. I thought to myself, "Well, this changes everything."

"I'm against picketing, but I don't know how to show it." -Mitch Hedberg

"For the amateur, the funniest thing in the world is the sight of a man dressed up as an old woman rolling down a steep hill in a wheelchair and crashing into a wall at the bottom of it. But to make a pro laugh, it would have to be a real old woman." -Groucho Marx

"Health nuts are going to feel stupid someday, lying in hospitals dying of nothing." -Redd Foxx

"Vegetables are a must on a diet. I suggest carrot cake, zucchini bread, and pumpkin pie." -Garfield

"My heroes are Larry Bird, Admiral Byrd, Lady Bird, Sheryl Crow, Chick Corea, the inventor of bird seed, and anyone who reads to you even if she's tired." -Big Bird

Social Media Silliness

"I changed all my passwords to "incorrect". So whenever I forget, it will tell me, "Your password is incorrect." -Comedy Tweets

"I needed a password eight characters long so I picked Snow White and the Seven Dwarves." -Nick Helm

"Social media's kind of like cotton candy. It looks so appealing, and you just can't resist getting in there – and then you end up with sticky fingers, and it lasted an instant." -Julia Roberts

"I don't believe in e-mail. I'm an old-fashioned girl. I prefer calling and hanging up." -Sarah Jessica Parker, in *Sex and the City*

tweet

Little Johnny @LittleJohnny1n2
Whoever stole my copy of Microsoft Office is in big trouble. You have my Word.

My boss texted me, "Send me one of your best jokes."

I answered, "I'm working right now...will send you one later."

He replied, "Terrific! Can you send me another?"

"Because Google is so popular, it's conceited. Have you tried misspelling something lately? See the tone that it takes? 'Um, did you mean ...?'"
-Arj Barker

"I hope cell phones aren't bad for us, but I would like the excuse: 'I can't talk right now. You're giving me cancer.'" -Whitney Cummings

Q Who's the patron saint of e-mail?

A: St. Francis of a CC.

Bathroom Break

What did one toilet say to the other toilet?

You look a little flushed.

"Personally, I'm waiting for caller IQ."
-Sandra Bernhard

"Any sufficiently advanced technology is indistinguishable from magic."
-Arthur C. Clarke

"I took a two-year-old computer in to be repaired, and the guy looked at me as though he was a gun dealer and I'd brought him a musket. In two years, I'd gone from cutting-edge to Amish."
-Jon Stewart

"The population of earth has reached seven billion people, every single one of whom send you irritating emails to join something called 'LinkedIn.'" -Dave Barry

"For every action there is an equal and opposite reaction, plus social media overreaction."
-Anonymous

Hey, you have something on your chin... no, the third one down.

Insta SLAM

Snap a picture of the slam, upload to Instagram with #instaslam and tag friends you want to diss

"You know you had a good night when you have to Google map yourself in the morning to find out where the hell you are." -Anonymous

A inmate was sitting in jail talking to his buddy on a phone. "Man! Reception is lousy," said his buddy. "How many bars do you have in your cell?"

"What I need is a search engine that, no matter what I type in, comes back with GO BACK TO WORK." -Dave Barry

"We had the Greatest Generation, the Boomers, Generation X, Generation Y, and now: Generation Text." -Greg Tamblyn

"Cars will soon have the Internet on the dashboard. I worry that this will distract me from my texting." -Andy Borowitz

"'User' is the word used by the computer professional when they mean 'idiot.'" -Dave Barry

What if .. One day Google was deleted and we couldn't Google what happened to Google...
-found on plus.google.com

It was a frigid winter morning when a woman sent this text to her husband, who had already left for work: "Windows frozen."

A little bit later, he sent this reply: "Pour lukewarm water over it."

Soon afterwards, she replied: "Computer is completely messed up now."

tweet

Little Johnny @LittleJohnny1n2
I named my dog "Five Miles" so I can tell people that I walk five miles every day.

"Respect your parents. They graduated school without Google or Wikipedia." -Anonymous

10 Facts About You

1. You're reading this right now.
2. You're realizing that is a stupid fact.
4. You didn't notice I skipped three.
5. You're checking now.
6. You're smiling.
7. You're still reading this even though it's stupid.
9. You didn't realize I skipped eight.
10. You're checking again and smiling about how you fell for it again.
11. You're enjoying this.
12. You didn't realize there's only supposed to be ten facts.

-Funny Quotes
for Instagram

Bathroom Break

Multi-Tasking: Flushing while you're talking on your cell -on a T-shirt

Do you know the most tech-savvy Israeli Prime Minister?

Netandyahoo

"I no longer keep a naughty or nice list. I'm only concerned with who friends me." -Santa Claus

"The difficult thing with quotes on the Internet is verifying them." -Abraham Lincoln

"A computer once beat me at chess, but it was no match for me at kickboxing." -Emo Philips

"I finally convinced my mother that it was a good idea for her to learn to text. Her first message to me: 'Whereisthespacebar?'" -Cindy Rose

tweet

Little Johnny @LittleJohnny1n2
Whatever you do in life, always give 100%- unless you're donating blood.

How did the mermaid and the fisherman meet?

Online

What do you get when you cross a rabbit with the Internet?

A hare net

What do you get when you cross a stomach with a cell phone?

A belly ring

What do skunks use to call each other?

Smell phones

Bertha: Do you have Facebook?

Harold: No

Bertha: Do you have Twitter?

Harold: No

Bertha: Do you have Instagram?

Harold: No

Bertha: Then what do you have!?!

Harold: A life.

Q & A

What do you get when you cross a hospital with a skunk?

A medical scenter.

What is the difference between congressmen and ex-cons?

Every so often, ex-cons pass a few good bills.

What did the mother deer say to the other deer?

Time flies when you are having fawn.

What do French people yell on roller coasters?

Yes!

tweet

Little Johnny @LittleJohnny1n2
When Miley Cyrus is naked and licks a hammer, it's "art." But when I do it, I'm "wasted" and have to leave Home Depot.

What do you get when a Mac falls off a desk?

Apple turnover.

What do you get when you drop a piano on an army base?

A flat major.

Why did the Siamese twins move to London?

So the other one could drive.

What happened when the computer fell on the floor?

It slipped a disk.

What is the difference between a trampoline and a lawyer?

You take your shoes off to jump on a trampoline.

What do you call a dog that hears voices?

A Shih-Tzu-Phrenic.

What do you get when you cross a centipede with a turkey?

Drumsticks for everyone!

Where do milkshakes come from?

Excited cows.

Twitter Twalk

"Did you know it's possible to Tweet a concise, grammatical, correctly punctuated sentence that is exactly one hundred forty characters long?"
-Steve Martin (go ahead- count 'em)

"Give a man a fish, and he will eat for a day. Give a man Twitter, and he will forget to eat and starve to death." -Andy Borowitz

•

Patient: Doc, you gotta help me. I'm addicted to Twitter!

Shrink: Sorry, I don't follow you.

•

What did the general do when he heard via Twitter that his troops were in trouble?

He retweeted.

tweet

Little Johnny @LittleJohnny1n2
I changed my iPhone's name to Titanic. It's syncing now.

Siri Says...

Even if you don't own an iPhone, chances are you
know about Siri, that sassy voice-powered assistant
who can give a plausible answer to almost any
question. Here are some entertaining ones
that Siri has handled.

Q: Will you talk dirty to me?

A: Okay, the carpet needs vacuuming.

Q: Why did the chicken cross the road?

A: I am not perspicacious about the
peregrinations of poultry.

Q: Mirror, mirror on the wall, who's the fairest of
them all?

A: Snow White?...Is that you?

Q: Do you like golf?

A: Not since that unfortunate javelin incident.

Q: Do you like football?

A: I'm not a fan of the old pigskin. Though I hear
bacon is pretty good.

Q: Can you tell me a poem?

A: Roses are red, violets are blue,
   Haven't you got anything better to do?

God & Google

Call it the Super-Information Highway
to Heaven. Here are actual messages posted
outside churches across the land.
As God would say, "Well, you did ask for a sign."

Claude Presbyterian Church

THERE ARE SOME QUESTIONS THAT CAN'T BE ANSWERED BY GOOGLE

tweet

Little Johnny @LittleJohnny1n2
I wrote a song about a tortilla.
Well actually, it's more of a wrap.

United New Church of Christ

WHY PAY FOR GPS?
JESUS GIVES
DIRECTION FOR FREE

• • •

St. Giles Presbyterian Church

You Have One New
Friend Request
From Jesus

Confirm   **Ignore**

• • •

Baptist Fall Creek Church

GET OFF OF FACEBOOK
AND INTO MY BOOK

Bathroom Break

Patient- Doc, I have a terrible problem.
I can't hold my water. I don't know
when I'm gonna pee. What do I do?

Doctor- Get off my carpet.

Stonebridge Church of God

HONK IF YOU LOVE JESUS
TEXT WHILE DRIVING
IF YOU WANT TO MEET HIM

• • •

New Madrid Baptist Church

IPOD, IPAD? TRY IPRAY
GOD IS LISTENING

• • •

GOOGLE DOES NOT
SATISFY
EVERY SEARCH

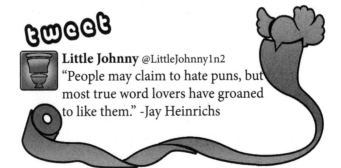

tweet

Little Johnny @LittleJohnny1n2
"People may claim to hate puns, but most true word lovers have groaned to like them." -Jay Heinrichs

Post-A-Joke

A guy goes to work with both ears bandaged and his boss says, "What happened to you?"

"I was pressing a shirt when the phone rang and I accidentally answered the iron."

"That explains one ear, but what about the other?"

"Well, I had to call the doctor."

A lawyer wakes up in the hospital after hours of delicate surgery. He looks around the dimly lit room and says, "Hey, Doc, how come the blinds are drawn?"

The doctors answers, "There's a big fire across the street. We didn't want you to think the operation was a failure."

A doctor examines a woman, then goes into the waiting room and says to the husband, "I don't want to scare you, but I don't like the way your wife looks."

The husband says, "Me neither, but she's a wonderful cook and is good with the kids."

Your selfie didn't come out quite right. You can still see your face.

𝓘𝓷𝓼𝓽𝓪 SLAM

Snap a picture of the slam, upload to Instagram with #instaslam and tag friends you want to diss

A husband and wife have been shopping for hours when the wife notices that her spouse has disappeared.

She calls him on his cell phone and says, "Where have you gone?"

He responds, "Darling, you know that jewelry store where I promised you I'd buy you that gorgeous diamond necklace you always wanted?"

She excitedly answers, "Yes, Dear! Yes!!"

He says, "Well, I'm having a beer at the bar next door."

A panhandler approached a well-dressed woman who was shopping on Fifth Avenue and said, "I haven't eaten anything in six days."

She responded, "God, I wish I had your willpower."

Bathroom Break

How many men does it take to put down a toilet seat?

Who knows -- it's never been done.

Bertha: Doc, you gotta do something about my husband. He thinks he's a refrigerator.

Shrink: I wouldn't worry about it if I were you. Lots of people have harmless temporary delusions. He'll probably get over it.

Bertha: Maybe you wouldn't worry about it, but I can't take it. He sleeps with his mouth open and the little light keeps me awake.

A couple had been dating for quite some time and the girl's birthday was coming up. "What would you like for your big day, Sweetheart?"

"Surprise me with a diamond," she said.

So he gave her a deck of cards.

Little Johnny @LittleJohnny1n2
Are there any medium rappers? They're always big or 'lil.

A guy goes to the circus and says to the ringmaster, "I do great bird impressions."

The ringmaster says, "That's nothing special, lots of people can do great bird impressions. Scram!"

The guy says, "Okay," and flies away.

A chicken was just about to cross the road when one of his cronies tried to warn him, "Don't do it. You'll never hear the end of it."

Two guys are out hunting at the lake when one of them bags a duck. Instantly, his Golden Retriever walks on top of the lake to fetch the duck.

"That's unbelievable!" his hunting buddy says. "Your dog just walked on water! Amazing!!"

"Ah, not really," says the first hunter. "He can't swim."

Oscar noticed that his buddy Gaylord had become despondent lately. "Cheer up, pal. You may think you have money problems, but I knew a guy who owed five grand that he couldn't pay. He wound up driving his vehicle to the edge of a cliff, where he sat for a long, long time. A group of citizens were very concerned about his problem so they passed a hat around. When all was said and done, the man backed away from the edge of the cliff."

"Wow," said Gaylord. "Who were these good Samaritans?"

"The passengers on the bus."

What's the first sign that a computer's getting old?

Loss of memory.

tweet

Little Johnny @LittleJohnny1n2
It's better to beat a dead horse than a live one.

A farmer's dog is missing and the old man is beside himself. His wife advises him to take out an ad in the newspaper so he does. But a couple of weeks later, there's still no sign of his faithful friend.

"What did you put in the ad?" the wife asks.

The farmer answers, "Here boy."

Knock Knock.

Who's there?

To.

To who?

No, to whom.

Bathroom Break

Do the people on Twitter really care how many times you went to the bathroom today?

A woman is driving in the wrong direction up a one-way street. A cop stops her and says, "Where do you think you are going?"

She says, "I don't know, but I think I'm late. Everyone's coming back!"

Patient: Doc, help me. I feel like I'm a bridge.

Doctor: Gosh! What's come over you?

Patient: Doc, I feel like I'm a small bucket.

Doctor: Well, you do look a little pail.

tweet

Little Johnny @LittleJohnny1n2
My girlfriend told me I was one in a million. After looking at her text messages, I found out she was right.

Patient: Doc, help me. I've got a strawberry growing out of my head.

Doctor: I'll give you some cream to put on it.

A music teacher said to his student, "You should have taken up singing earlier."

The encouraged pupil replied, "You mean I'd be even further along with my talent?"

"No. You might have quit by now."

As the casket is being carried out after a woman's funeral service, the pallbearers bump into a wall. The husband hears a faint moan, opens the casket and finds out that his wife is still alive!

Ten years later, the woman dies "again" and another funeral is held. After the service, as the casket is being carried toward the door, the husband shouts, "Watch out for the wall!"

A man goes to a doctor for a physical. The doctor is astonished when he finds money stuffed into one of the guy's ears. He removes the money, counts it, and says, "Wow, there's exactly $1,900 here."

The guy says, "I knew I wasn't feeling two grand."

Husband: Doctor! Doctor! My wife is in labor and she keeps screaming, "Shouldn't, wouldn't, couldn't!"

Doctor: Don't be alarmed. She's just having contractions.

tweet

Little Johnny @LittleJohnny1n2
Vegetarians, if you love animals so much then why do you keep eating all their food?

A married couple were in a horrible accident where the wife's face was severely burned. The doctor told her that they couldn't graft skin from her body because she was too thin. The husband offered to donate some of his own skin and the doctor advised that it would have to come from his buttocks.

Arrangements were made for the operation, the surgery took place and the result was a resounding success. The wife looked as radiant as ever, her face not revealing one iota of the ordeal she'd experienced.

She was overcome with emotion and said to her husband, "Dear, I can't possibly thank you enough for the sacrifice you made."

"Honey," he answered, "I get all the thanks I need every time I see your mother kiss you on the cheek."

Bathroom Break

Apple co-founder Steve Wozniak is a practical joker. On one of his many plane trips, he posted official-looking foil labels on the doors of the plane's lavatories which read, "Do Not Flush Over Cities."

A cop wrote out a speeding ticket. The recipient angrily began waving it in the air and said, "What am I supposed to do with this?"

"Keep it," said the cop. "When you collect three more, you get a bicycle."

Two surgeons were laughing hysterically in a hospital hallway when a dermatologist walked by and asked, "What's so funny?"

One of the surgeons answered, "You wouldn't understand. It's an inside joke."

tweet

Little Johnny @LittleJohnny1n2
If life gives you melons, you're probably dyslexic.

A cop stops a driver on the interstate and says, "Sir, the back lights on your car are defective."

The driver gets out of his vehicle, looks toward the back of the car and begins sobbing uncontrollably.

"Oh, c'mon, mister. It's not that bad," says the cop.

"Oh no? Then would you mind telling me where my trailer and boat are?"

A woman is standing before the judge in a packed courtroom.

The judge asks, "What is it that you stole from the grocery store, ma'am?"

"Only a small can of a half dozen peaches," pleaded the woman.

"That'll be six nights in jail- one night for each stolen peach," declares the judge.

The woman is crestfallen. She looks like she's just about to faint when her husband shouts out from the back of the courtroom, "She stole a can of peas too!"

Mrs. Jones was instructing her second-grade class when she said, "Give me a sentence using the words fireman and ladder."

She called on Little Johnny, who answered, "The fireman came down the ladder pregnant."

"Do you know what pregnant means?" asked the teacher.

"Of course," Johnny said. "It means carrying a child."

A guy walks into a lumberyard and asks for some two-by-fours. The clerk asks, "How long do you need them?"

The guy answers, "A long time. We're gonna build a house."

twEEt

Little Johnny @LittleJohnny1n2
My parents accused me of lying today.
I said, "Tooth Fairy, Easter Bunny and Santa Claus," and walked away.

Little Johnny's riding with his mother when they pull up to a stoplight alongside another car. Johnny peers over and can't believe his eyes as he sees a totally naked woman in the driver's seat.

"Well will you look at that, ma!" Johnny says. "That lady's not wearing a seat belt!"

A woman buys a super duper high-tech coffeemaker with every gizmo imaginable. The salesman tells her how to work it, from plugging it in to filling it up and setting the timer so that she'll wake up to a fresh cup of coffee every day.

After a couple of weeks, she returns to the store and complains to the salesman, "You know, this coffeemaker is great, but there's just one thing. Why do I have to go to bed every time I make a cup of coffee?"

Bathroom Break

"I walk into rooms and I don't know why I'm there. I'm like, 'Why am I standing in front of the toilet now?'"
-Matthew Broderick

Knock Knock?

Who's there?

Madonna

Madonna who?

That's showbiz.

"How do you spell the word 'straight'?" asked Mrs. Jones, to her third grade class.

From the back of the room, Little Johnny answered, "S-T-R-A-I-G-H-T."

"Excellent," remarked the teacher. "And what does that mean, Johnny?"

"Without ice."

Why don't you slip into something more comfortable- like a coma!

Insta SLAM

Snap a picture of the slam, upload to Instagram with #instaslam and tag friends you want to diss

The preacher at a revival meeting asks for anyone who needs prayer to please stand up and state their problem. Herb does so and says, "I need prayers for my hearing."

With that, the preacher approaches Herb, puts a hand around each of his ears and begins praying. When he's done, he says, "How's your hearing now?"

Herb says, "I dunno. I don't go to court until next week."

There's a knock on the door of the Pearly Gates. St. Peter answers it and sees a guy there. St. Peter turns around to lead him in to his eternal bliss but the fellow disappears.

In a few moments, there's another knock. St. Peter answers it. It's the same guy. And as soon as St. Peter sees him, he vanishes again.

A bit later, there's another knock. St. Peter answers it one more time, sees the same guy, and says, "What is this, some kind of game you're playing?"

The guy answers, "No, they're trying to resuscitate me."

A man takes his Dachshund to the vet and says, "My dog is cross-eyed. Is there anything you can do for him?"

The vet says, "Well, let's have a look."

The vet picks the dog up and examines his eyes. Finally he says, "I'm going to have to put him down."

"What?" the man protested in horror. "Just because he's cross-eyed?"

"No," replied the vet, "because he's really, really heavy."

What's the opposite of irony?

Wrinkly

tweet

Little Johnny @LittleJohnny1n2
For sale: Baby shoes, never worn.

"That young couple next door is so lovely," says Ethel to her husband. "In the morning, when he leaves the house, he kisses her goodbye, and every evening he comes home with flowers. Why can't you do something sweet like that?"

"Because I don't even know her."

A guy visits the doctor because he has excruciating pain in his leg. The doctor examines him with a stethoscope and hears a tiny voice coming from his kneecap. The voice keeps saying, "Lend us a dollar, lend us a dollar…"

"My ankle is killing me too," says the guy.

The doctor listens with his stethoscope and hears a little voice coming from the ankle. It, too, says, "Lend us a dollar, lend us a dollar…"

The doctor says, "This is not good. Your leg is broke in two places."

Bathroom Break

"What did people do when they went to the bathroom before smart phones?"
-Aaron Cobra

Little Johnny asks his mother her age. She replies, "Gentlemen don't ask a lady how old she is."

Johnny then asks his mother how much she weighs. His mother once again answers, "Gentlemen don't ask ladies that question."

Johnny then asks, "Why did Daddy leave you?"

His mother says, "You shouldn't ask that."

A bit later, Johnny gets into some mischief. Rummaging through his mother's purse, he comes across her driver's license. He runs up to his mother and excitedly says, "I know all about you now. You're 35 years old, you weigh 125 pounds and Daddy left you because you got an 'F' in sex!"

Tweet

Little Johnny @LittleJohnny1n2
There are 364 days until Christmas and people already have their Christmas lights up. Unbelievable.

One Sunday morning in church, Little Johnny said, "Mommy, I gotta pee."

His mother said, "It's not polite to say the word 'pee' in church. From now on, if you have to pee, just say that you have to 'whisper.'"

The next week, Johnny was in church with his father when he said, "Daddy, I have to whisper."

His dad said, "Okay, just whisper in my ear."

What's blue and smells like red paint?

Blue paint

A tour guide was showing a vacationer around Washington, D.C. The guide pointed out the place where George Washington supposedly threw a silver dollar across the Potomac River.

"That's impossible," said the tourist. "No one could throw a coin that far!"

"You have to remember," answered the guide. "A dollar went a lot farther in those days."

A New Yorker calls his mother who lives in Florida. She answers the phone with a very weak-sounding voice.

"Mom, you don't sound good. What's wrong?"

Very feebly she answers, "I haven't eaten in quite some time."

"How long has it been Mom?"

"My last meal was 26 days ago."

"26 days! How come?"

"I didn't want to be caught with food in my mouth when you called."

tweet

Little Johnny @LittleJohnny1n2
I tried water polo but my horse drowned.

Frank was sitting in a men's room stall minding his own business when a guy occupied the next stall over. All of a sudden Frank heard, "Hello, how are you doing?"

"Er, ah, well, okay I guess," said Frank, who was not used to carrying on conversations with strangers in public bathrooms.

"How long are you planning to stay?"

"Geez, a couple more minutes I guess," Frank stammered in response.

"Having any problems?" the voice asked.

"Certainly not!" responded Frank, a bit indignantly.

Then the other fellow said, "Look, Charlie I'll call you back. Whenever I say anything, the idiot in the next stall keeps answering me!"

Bathroom Break

"Two heads are better than one- unless you're cleaning them."
-Craig Sharf

A guy was shopping for dinner at a supermarket when a beautiful redhead smiled and waved at him. He couldn't figure out where he knew her from but nonetheless he was thrilled at the attention until she walked up and said, "I think you're the father of one of my kids."

Taken aback, he initially denied it but then he searched his memory. "Wait a minute," he blurted out. "That night my buddies got me drunk and took all my clothes and set me out on Main Street and I wandered around until I came into this little bar and fell in the mud-wrestling pit and vomited all over the floor... Were you the stripper who took me home with her that night?"

"No," she answered coolly. "I'm your son's math teacher."

tweet

Little Johnny @LittleJohnny1n2
Sometimes I text and drive. I know it's dangerous, but I do stupid things when I'm drunk.

A pair of elderly couples were chatting at dinner when one of the husbands said, "Bentley, how was that memory clinic you went to last week?"

"Great," answered Bentley. "We were taught all the latest and greatest memory helpers - association, visualization - that kind of stuff."

"Sounds good ... I might like to take a class. What was the name of it?"

Bentley's mind went blank. Then he suddenly smiled and said, "What do you call that flower that's red with a long stem and thorns?"

His buddy said, "You mean a rose?"

Bentley said, "Yeah, that's it," then turned to his wife and asked, "What was the name of that memory clinic, Rose?"

What do you call twin police officers?

Copies

Why did Beethoven get rid of his chicken?

It kept saying, "Bach, Bach, Bach, Bach, Bach..."

A woman visits an art gallery and sees two very similar still-life paintings, both of a table spread out for lunch and both portraying a glass of wine, a basket of bread rolls and a plate of sliced ham. One painting, however, is selling for $100 and the other for $75.

The woman is curious about the price differential and asks the gallery owner about it. The owner responds, "You get more ham with the $100 painting."

Doctor: I haven't seen you in quite a while.

Patient: I know. I've been ill.

tweet

Little Johnny @LittleJohnny1n2
What's up with "Fun sized" candy? There is nothing fun about less candy.

A driver runs over a cat. The cat's collar has its address, so the driver goes to the owner's house. He knocks on the door and a little old lady answers. The apologetic guy says, "I'm so very sorry. I've just run over your cat. Can I replace it?"

The old lady answers, "I'm not sure. Are you any good at catching mice?"

The hysterical woman charged into the police station screaming that her car had been stolen.

"Calm down, ma'am," advised the desk sergeant. "Do you have a description of the suspect?"

"No," the woman replied, fighting back tears, "but I did manage to get the license plate number."

Bathroom Break

Why can't you hear a Pterodactyl going to the bathroom?

Because the P is silent.

Three old geezers were sitting on a city park bench. The one in the middle was reading a newspaper while the other two were pretending to fish.

A policeman on the beat watched them as they baited imaginary hooks, cast their lines and reeled in their fake catches.

"Do you know these two?" the cop asked the guy reading the paper.

"Sure. They're buddies of mine."

"Well, they're disturbin' the other people. You better get them outta here!"

"Yes, officer," said the guy, and with that he put down his newspaper and furiously began rowing.

tweet

Little Johnny @LittleJohnny1n2
I have CDO. It's like OCD, but the letters are in alphabetical order, LIKE THEY SHOULD BE.

A husband and wife are awakened at two in the morning by a knock at the front door. The husband gets up and goes to the door, where a stranger is asking for a push.

"No way," says the husband. "It's two a.m.!"

He closes the door and returns to bed. His wife asks, "Who was that?"

"Just a stranger asking for a push."

"Did you give him one?"

The husband answers, "No, I didn't. It's two a.m."

"You must have a short memory," says the wife. "Four months ago our car broke down and two guys helped us then. Can't you help him now?"

The husband thinks better of it, goes to the front door and calls out into the dark, "Hello - excuse me - are you still there?"

"Yes, I'm here."

"Do you still want a push?" asks the husband.

"Yes, yes, please!"

"Well, where are you?"

"I'm over here on the hammock."

Charlie hadn't been feeling well so he went to his doctor for a complete checkup. Afterward, the doctor came out with the results.

"I'm afraid I have some very bad news," the doctor said. "You're dying, and you don't have much time left."

"Oh, that's terrible!" moaned Charlie. "Tell me, Doc. How much longer do I have?"

"Ten," the doctor said sadly.

"Ten?" Charlie asked. "Ten what? Months? Weeks? What?"

"Nine..."

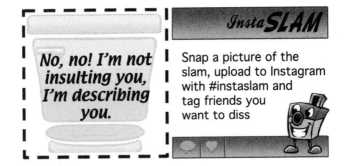

No, no! I'm not insulting you, I'm describing you.

*Insta*SLAM

Snap a picture of the slam, upload to Instagram with #instaslam and tag friends you want to diss

A husband was troubled that his wife was experiencing some hearing loss so he sought the advice of a physician. The doctor suggested a simple test to determine if, indeed, there was a problem.

When the fellow returned home that evening, his wife was preparing dinner at the stove. "Hi, Dear," he said in a normal tone of voice. "What's for dinner?"

No answer.

He took a few steps closer to his bride, as the doctor had suggested for this test, and then repeated, "What's for dinner?"

Still no response.

Then he moved directly behind her and shouted, "What's for dinner?"

His wife spun around and loudly exclaimed, "For the third time - pot roast! What are you, deaf!?!"

Bathroom Break

Why does toilet paper need a commercial? Is there anyone not buying this?

The Name Game

What do you call a guy buried in a garden?

Pete

What do you call a guy under a car?

Jack

What do you call a guy in a catapult?

Chuck

What do you call a guy in a pile of leaves?

Russell

What do you call an Italian guy with a rubber toe?

Roberto

tweet

Little Johnny @LittleJohnny1n2
All my life I thought air was free-
until I bought a bag of chips.

A minister, priest, and a rabbi get together weekly for a small stakes game of poker. The local police learn that they're doing some gambling and one night raid their game. They're taken to the hoosegow and appear before a judge in front of a packed courtroom the next morning.

The judge looks at the priest and says, "Father, I hear you've been doing some gambling. Is this true?"

The priest mutters to God to please forgive him for the white lie he's about to tell, then says, "Why, no ... of course not, your Honor."

The judge says, "Okay, you're free to go, Father," then turns to the minister and says, "Reverend, is it true that you've been gambling?"

The minister also asks forgiveness from God before saying, "No, I haven't been gambling, your honor."

The judge excuses the minister and asks the rabbi, "Have you been gambling?"

The rabbi answers, "With who?"

An elderly fellow goes to his doctor and complains that he hears music every time he wears his hat. The doctor takes that hat, goes into another room with it and comes back a few moments later. "Here, try the hat on now," advises the doctor.

The old guy puts the hat on and says, "Incredible. I don't hear music anymore. What did you do to the hat?"

"Simple," says the good doctor. "I removed the band."

Why did the Amish couple divorce?

Because he was driving her buggy.

tweet

Little Johnny @LittleJohnny1n2
I need to start a diet. I stepped on the scale and it said, "I need your weight, not your phone number."

Herb is telling Tim about the brand new thermos he brought along for their camping trip. "It's great," he said. "The guy at the store where I bought it told me it keeps hot things hot and cold things cold."

"Sweet," said Tim. "What do you have in it?"

"Three coffees and an ice cream sandwich."

A guy goes to a police station to file a report on his missing wife. The officer filling out the report asks the husband to describe her.

"Alright," says the hubby, "but on one condition. You can't show her the report afterward."

Bathroom Break

The amount of time it takes for a minute to go by is proportionally dependent with the distance to the bathroom door. -coolfunnyquotes.com

An elderly man was at home on his deathbed. He smelled the aroma of his favorite cookies baking. He craved for one last chocolate chip cookie before he died.

He fell out of bed, crawled to the landing, then down the stairs and finally to the kitchen where his wife was baking. With waning strength he made his way to the table and was just barely able to lift his arm to the cookie sheet. As he grasped a warm, moist cookie, his wife suddenly whacked his hand with a spatula.

"Why," he meekly and weakly said, "did you do that?"

She replied, "Because they're for the funeral."

tweet

Little Johnny @LittleJohnny1n2
When you get a bladder infection, urine trouble.

Once upon a time there were three storks: Papa Stork, Mama Stork, and Baby Stork. One evening, Mama Stork had prepared a meal, but Papa Stork didn't come home at all that night.

The next day, Baby Stork said, "Papa, where were you last night?"

Papa Stork answered, "I was out making a married couple very, very happy."

The next week, it was Mama Stork who didn't come home one night. Papa Stork and Baby Stork wound up ordering out for pizza.

The next morning Baby Stork asked Mama Stork, "Where were you last night?"

Mama Stork said, "I was out making a married couple very, very happy."

A few weeks later, Baby Stork was late for dinner. They waited and waited, but Baby Stork didn't come home until the wee hours of the next morning.

"And where were you all night?" Papa Stork demanded.

"I was out scaring the crap out of a couple of college students."

Sam and Moe were rocking on a porch in the blistering heat of Miami Beach. Having talked about everything under the sun during their long friendship, Sam was grasping for a new topic of conversation.

"Tell me, Moe, have you read Marx?" Sam asked.

"Yes," replied Moe. "And you know, I think it's these wicker chairs."

What's big and gray and wrote depressing poetry?

T.S. Elephant

Clones are people two.

tweet

Little Johnny @LittleJohnny1n2
I used to think the brain was the most important organ. Then I thought, look what's telling me that.

Ralph forgot his wedding anniversary and his wife was more than a bit agitated. "Tomorrow morning, I expect to find a gift in the driveway that goes from 0 to 200 in five seconds. And it better be there or else!" she yelled.

The next morning Ralph woke up early to do his thing. When his wife got up, she looked out the window and sure enough there was a gift-wrapped box, smack in the middle of the driveway.

The wife put on her robe and slippers, ran outside and opened it up right then and there – a bathroom scale.

What's the difference between a guy and a dog running?

One wears trousers and the other pants.

Bathroom Break

Confucius say man who smoke weed on toilet is high on pot.

An artist asked the gallery owner if there had been any interest in his paintings.

"Good news and bad news," said the owner. "A fellow asked about your work and wondered if it would appreciate in value after your death. When I assured him that it would, he bought all twelve of your paintings."

"Wonderful," said the artist. "What could the bad news possibly be?"

"He was your doctor."

Q: What kind of coffee was served on the Titanic?

A: Sanka.

tweet

Little Johnny @LittleJohnny1n2
I'm on a beer diet. I've lost three days already.

A savvy antiques collector was walking through an artsy section of San Francisco when he noticed a mangy old cat lapping milk from a saucer in the doorway of a ceramic shop. He recognized instantly that the saucer was a sought-after piece missing from the estate of George Washington and a veritable national treasure, so he entered the store and slyly offered to buy the cat for ten dollars.

The owner said, "Sorry, it's not for sale."

"Please, I have an awful problem with mice around my house. I could use the old tomcat to catch them. I'll tell you what. I'll double my offer for him."

The owner shot back, "Twenty dollars it is. He's all yours."

The collector picked up the cat and said, "I wonder if you'll throw in that old saucer with it. I noticed the cat drinking out of it and it'll save me from having to buy another dish."

"Nothing doing buddy," the owner replied. "That's my lucky saucer. So far I've sold 62 cats."

A guy is standing on the curb, about to cross the road. As soon as he steps down onto the street, a car heads straight at him. He moves faster, but so does the vehicle. The guy thinks better of going across the street and moves quickly back, but the car changes lanes and is heading right for him.

The guy freezes right in the middle of the road and the car comes screeching to a halt. The driver rolls down the window. Behind the wheel is a squirrel. "See," the squirrel says, "it's not as easy as it looks, is it?"

Q: What do you feed an invisible cat?

A: Evaporated milk

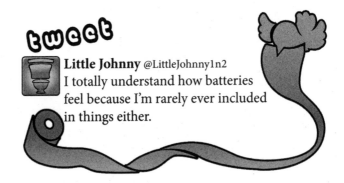

tweet

Little Johnny @LittleJohnny1n2
I totally understand how batteries feel because I'm rarely ever included in things either.

A crowd of husbands are about to enter through the Pearly Gates when St. Peter roars, "Hold it right there! I want all of you who were henpecked husbands while on Earth to form a line to my right. The rest of you stand to my left."

All but one husband stands on the henpecked line. St. Peter turns to the guy standing alone and says, "How about you? What's your story?"

He replies sheepishly, "My wife told me to stand here."

"Hey, Grandpa, can you make a noise like a frog?" asked Little Johnny.

"Why do you want me to do that, Johnny?"

"Because Mom said when you croak, we're goin' to Disney World!"

Bathroom Break

No matter how bad your day seems, just remember that someone out there has to clean the bathroom at Taco Bell.
-your ecards

Little Johnny was in his kindergarten class when the teacher asked the kids what their dads did for a living. The usual jobs came up- fireman, salesman, accountant, policeman- but Johnny was uncharacteristically shy about giving an answer.

Finally, the teacher said, "Johnny, how about you? What does your father do for a living?"

Johnny murmured, "My dad's a circus freak who bites the heads off small animals."

The startled teacher quickly ended that segment of class and sent the other kids off to do some coloring. Then she took little Johnny aside and said, "Is that really true about your father?"

"No," said Johnny, "but I was afraid the other kids would make fun of me if I said that he's really a lawyer."

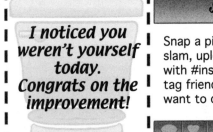

I noticed you weren't yourself today. Congrats on the improvement!

InstaSLAM

Snap a picture of the slam, upload to Instagram with #instaslam and tag friends you want to diss

A guy applies for a sales position with a big financial investment firm. While he's waiting for the interview, he strikes up a conversation with the receptionist, who at one point says, "Look, you seem like a nice guy. Let me give you a tip. My boss is very sensitive about the fact that he doesn't have any ears. At some point, he's going to ask you if you notice anything odd about him. Whatever you do, don't make any mention of the ears."

The guy thanks the receptionist for the advice and goes in for the interview. Well, the boss is very impressed with the guy's resume, his knowledge of the world of finance and his personable demeanor. But sure enough, at one point the boss says, "Tell me. Do you notice anything different about me?"

The guy looks at the boss and responds, "Well, now that you mention it, I can tell you're wearing contact lenses."

"That's amazing," says the boss. "I like perceptiveness in my employees. But how on earth did you know I wear contacts?"

"Easy. You'd be wearing glasses if you had any ears."

Little Johnny's mother, in an attempt to get him to stop sucking his thumb, told him that if he continued to do so his stomach would get bigger and bigger until it burst.

Later that day they went to the supermarket, where Johnny saw a very pregnant woman. Noticing that he was staring at her, the woman said, "You don't know me. You shouldn't be staring at me."

Johnny replied, "I may not know you, but I know what you've been doing."

Q: What does an educated owl say?

A: "Whom."

tweet

Little Johnny @LittleJohnny1n2
Yawning is your body's way of saying 20% battery remaining.

A kindergarten teacher was reading the "Three Little Pigs" to her class. She came to the part of the story where the first pig was trying to gather the building materials for his home.

She read, "...And so the pig went up to the man with the wheelbarrow full of straw and said, 'Excuse me sir, but may I have some of that straw to build my house?'"

The teacher paused and then asked the class, "And what do you think that man said?"

Little Johnny raised his hand and said, "I know. He said, 'Holy crap! A talking pig!'"

And then there was the hillbilly couple that named their kids Bobby Joe, Billy Joe, Betty Lou, Betty Sue and Chung because they heard that every fifth child born in the world is Chinese.

Bathroom Break

Why do they call it the restroom? Is there anybody just resting in this room?

After receiving the diagnosis from his psychiatrist, the patient says, "Doc, I know you say I have a split personality, but is it okay for me to get married?"

"Sure ... Who are you planning to marry?"

"The Jones twins."

A guy goes to a psychiatrist and says, "My wife thinks I'm crazy because I like plaid socks."

"That's not so strange," replies the doctor. "As a matter of fact, I kind of like them, too."

"Really?" exclaimed the patient, excited to find a sympathetic ear. "Do you like yours with chocolate fudge or Hollandaise sauce?"

tweet

Little Johnny @LittleJohnny1n2
I accidentally called 911, so I set my house on fire so I wouldn't look stupid.

Harvey had been in and out of a coma for several months. His wife stayed by his side every moment. One evening he came to, and called her over to his bed.

She sat by him and tears welled up in her eyes as he said, "My darling, you were with me all along, always at my side. When I got fired, you were there. When I got charged with tax evasion, you were there. When my business went bankrupt, you were there. And now, my health is failing and you are here. You know what?"

"What my dear? Tell me what," she implored, her voice cracking with emotion.

Harvey drew his last gasp of air and replied, "I'm beginning to think you're bad luck."

Donald Trump visits an old folks' home to mingle with the people and pick up a little good P.R. at the same time. He walks up to a sweet old lady in a wheelchair who smiles at him with an otherwise blank stare. "Do you know who I am?" says The Donald.

She responds, "No, but if you ask at the desk, they'll tell you."

Farnsworth and his wife, Edith, were having breakfast one morning when the misses said, "You probably don't know what day this is, do you?"

"Of course I do," Farnsworth huffily replied as he got up to leave for work.

A couple of hours later, the doorbell rang. When Edith opened the door, she was presented with a dozen roses. Shortly after noon, there was another delivery. This time it was a box of her favorite chocolates. The doorbell rang again shortly after five, when an enormous fruit basket was delivered.

When Farnsworth came home, Edith excitedly said, "A dozen roses, a box of chocolates, and a beautiful fruit basket. This is the best Groundhog Day I've ever had!"

tweet

Little Johnny @LittleJohnny1n2
I'm friends with 25 letters in the alphabet. I don't know Y.

A rabbit hopped into a butcher shop and asked, "Do you have any carrots?"

"No," said the butcher.

The next day the rabbit showed up and said, "Have any carrots?"

"If I told you once, I told you twice- The answer is NO," said the butcher.

The following day the rabbit appeared again and said, "Got any carrots?"

The butcher angrily replied, "N-O, NO! And if you come back in here again and ask for carrots, I'll hammer you to the wall by your ears!"

The next day the rabbit came back and asked, "Do you have any nails?"

"No," said the butcher.

"Good ... Do you have any carrots?"

Bathroom Break

"Humor is a reminder that no matter how high the throne one sits on, one sits on one's bottom." -Taki

Four guys are fishing in a rowboat at the lake. A motorboat speeds by, the boat tips over and the fishermen are thrown into the water. They all swim ashore and take off their wet clothes to dry them over a fire.

Soon, two beautiful girls pass by on jet skis. The embarrassed guys wrap their jerseys around their loins – except for one of them, who wraps his shirt around his head and face. After the girls go by, one fisherman turns to the other and says, "What did you do that for?"

"Well, I don't know about you," he answers, "but the people I know usually recognize each other by their faces."

tweet

Little Johnny @LittleJohnny1n2
I invented a new word today called "plagiarism".

A fanatical fisherman calls his doctor and says, "Doc, you gotta help me out. It's an emergency. My baby swallowed a fish hook!"

The doctor says, "Bring him to my office. I'll meet you there."

Before the doctor can even get out the door, the phone rings again and the fisherman says, "Never mind, Doc. I found another fish hook."

A turtle was moseying across the road when he got mugged by a couple of snails. When the cop showed up and asked him what happened, the turtle said, "I don't know. It all happened so fast."

A psychiatrist is talking to the brother of one of his patients and says, "It would be wise to stay away from your brother for awhile. He has delusions of grandeur and thinks he's Brutus right now."

"What does that have to do with me?" asks the brother.

"He thinks you're Caesar."

A ventriloquist is telling a dumb-blonde joke when an offended platinum-haired woman in the audience yells out, "You have no right to stereotype blondes that way!!"

The ventriloquist becomes flustered and tries to apologize but she cuts him off, saying, "You stay out of this! I'm talking to that little twerp on your knee!"

Mabel tells Gertrude of her husband's untimely death. "Poor old Harold was out in the vegetable patch to get me some greens, when all of the sudden he dropped dead of a heart attack."

"Oh, my goodness. What a tragedy! Whatever did you do?" asks Gertrude.

"I had to defrost some string beans."

tweet

Little Johnny @LittleJohnny1n2
I was a schizophrenic, but we're all right now.

A traveling salesman came up to an old man rocking on his front porch but stopped short when he spotted a rather large and fierce looking dog. "Excuse me, sir," the salesman called out. "Does your dog bite?"

"Nope," the old man answered.

The salesman straightened his phony grin and confidently strode up the steps. With that, the dog jumped at him and buried his teeth in the salesman's backside.

"Hey, I thought you said your dog didn't bite," complained the salesman.

The old man looked up and said, "It ain't my dog."

Maybe you heard about the robbery at PBS television. The thieves made off with $50,000 in pledges.

Bathroom Break

"I have a very silly sense of humor. I've never laughed harder in my entire life than seeing someone with toilet paper stuck on the bottom of their shoe." -Paula Poundstone

An old fellow orders a bowl of soup at a restaurant. The waiter brings him the soup and starts to walk away. The old guy beckons to the waiter and says, "Taste this soup."

"Is it too hot?" the waiter asks.

The old man shakes his head. "Taste it."

The waiter asks, "Is it too cold?"

"Taste it," the senior responds.

"Is it too spicy?" the waiter asks.

"I said, taste the soup."

Now the waiter is totally exasperated. "Okay, okay, I'll taste it... Where's the spoon?"

"Ah-ha!" says the old man gleefully.

tweet

Little Johnny @LittleJohnny1n2
A friend of mine said his new girlfriend really takes his breath away. I'm guessing she's inflatable.